SACRED LIVING

Dedication

*In memory of my father
whose wisdom and integrity
graced our lives.*

Grace Clunie

Sacred Living

Practical inspirations from Celtic spirituality
for the contemporary spiritual journey

the columba press

First published in 2011 by
the columba press
55A Spruce Avenue, Stillorgan Industrial Park,
Blackrock, Co Dublin

Cover by Bill Bolger
Origination by The Columba Press
Printed in Ireland by Gemini International Limited

ISBN 978 1 85607 743 9

Contents

Foreword

The Centre for Celtic Spirituality is appropriately located in Armagh, the ecclesiastical capital of Ireland. Ard Macha is steeped in history, a lot of which is BCE (Before the Common Era). Before the Christian story arrived and there was any association with St Patrick, there was an Armagh story of sacredness and spirituality. Armagh models the continuity and discontinuity that is always part of the ongoing dynamic and constant change at the heart of life. There is therefore something visionary about a Centre for Celtic Spirituality in Armagh, and the vision that has driven and sustains this project is rooted in the mists and mystery of location. It also expresses the need to envisage a different future, not only for Ard Macha, but for all of Northern Ireland, and its relationships with the rest of Ireland as well as Irish-British relationships. The Centre draws on its deep spiritual history and brings the best of that rich past to bear on the challenge of peace and reconciliation in a society struggling to emerge from violent conflict, a product of our religious and political sectarianism.

The director of the Centre has written a rich introduction to Celtic spirituality, providing us with many insights into what inspires the work of the Centre. In a sense, here we have the spiritual rationale for the Centre's existence and its work of spiritual nurture, peace and reconciliation, not only between human beings, but also in the earth-human relationship. It is a book which is practical and experiential and draws us into the sense of otherness or sacredness at the heart of our personal and collective lives, as well as in creation itself.

I think it is significant that Grace Clunie begins and ends with personal stories. The stories provide the clues to Grace's own pilgrimage and what has drawn her into the Celtic story. There is much warmth about the story of being on the ancient hill of Navan on a freezing cold night. All the elements of Celtic spirituality are in it. The end story of her childhood years is filled with earthiness, simplicity and profundity. Growing up as she did with the natural rhythms of the earth's cycles, was, she acknowledges, foundational in drawing her into Celtic spirituality. I suspect that when Grace discovered Celtic spirituality, she discovered something she had always known.

Grace then takes us on a practical journey through the core elements of this ancient, yet perennial spirituality. It emerges from her book-end stories. And here is an experience of spirituality that 'has the potential to reconnect us with the Sacred Presence at the heart of life, with the rest of creation and with the beauty of our own authentic selves.'

This is experiential spirituality, practical and earthed. Helpfully at the end of each chapter we are invited to engage with individual and community exercises. Here we have spirituality for living and which combines being and doing. It is also a spirituality which engages the right side of the brain, the artistic and imaginative.

In a community where there are religious and political divisions, and much of the history of atrocity and violence go back to the sixteenth century, we are grateful for the possibility of getting in touch with a spirituality that is older than our sectarian divisions. This book is not, though, about going back to a pure past, which is impossible, not least because a pure past or a paradise lost has never existed. But it is about reconnecting with deep roots of ancient wisdom which can and do flow in fresh ways in our present. Such ancient wisdom can enable us to change the future, providing the inner resources for peacemaking and peacebuilding. Here indeed, is the invitation to 'follow the road less travelled'.

Dr Johnston McMaster
2011

Introduction

On a freezing cold night – 22 December 1987 – four people walked through the snow-frozen streets of the old city of Armagh. It was the night of the winter solstice and they wanted to mark the year's turning by walking to the ancient hill of Navan, a mile or so outside the city, a place once known as *Emain Macha*, seat of the Kings and Queens of Ulster. In 1987 it was a place frequented by few, an isolated, quiet hill that held within it the mysteries of centuries past.

The four people, two men and two women, were all from different backgrounds and held different views about life. One was French, one born in Africa, one Southern Irish, one Northern Irish, all friends.

As they left the street lights behind, the only sounds were the crunching of their feet through the dusty snow and the slow passing of an occasional vehicle. Climbing the snow-covered hill of Navan on that dark winter's night, you might ask, what were they doing? I can only say what my own thoughts were, for I was one of the four, and it's an experience I will always remember because it contained so many of the elements which were later to become central to my own perspective on life.

Firstly, there was the physical joy of being out in the icy beauty of that winter's evening, with the lights of the city far below us, feeling somehow remote from civilisation. Then there was the closeness of friendship – valued for no other reason than our shared respect for one another. There was also the sacred feel of the place – steeped in over 3,000 years of human experience; an ancient place representing the social and ritual practices of ancestors long gone. There was also the hope that in this ancient place, on this particular night at the end of the shortest day of the year, we might experience the 'Sacred Presence' and be enabled to pray for peace in Northern Ireland and for our own individual lives.

So, there we were, each standing in a chosen place, communing with our own hearts on the darkest night of the old year in the place of the ancestors – when the craziest thing happened! Suddenly we were surrounded by bright lights – a heavenly visitation? Well, no, not exactly.

A man's voice with a clear English accent called out of the darkness – 'Show yourselves ... Who's there?'

It was a British Army foot patrol – for in those days in the 1980s, Northern Ireland was still a very troubled and violent place.

That night our moment of sacred mystery was suddenly interrupted as we were escorted from the hill by the British Army patrol, with some amusement to them and to ourselves and those we told the story to later on.

I begin this book about Sacred Living with the sharing of this story because in so many ways it illustrates much that's at the heart of Celtic spirituality and which can also be applied to life in general.

It was an experience wrapped up in the beauty of nature: a sacred pilgrimage in the company of friends; an opportunity to perceive the sacred in all of life – not just the conventional 'holy' bits; a moment of awareness of the ancestors and of sacred times and places; a sacred experience which brought together people of different gender, religion and background – and at the same time as all of this – laughter, humour and joy along the way. All of this is also Celtic spirituality.

In those days back in the 1980s, long before my ordination or any knowledge of Celtic spirituality, the seeds of the future were already present. Now in Armagh City, since 2007, there is a Centre for Celtic Spirituality – a shared, charitable project with a desire for peace and reconciliation at its heart – peace with one another and with all of creation.

This book was written out of the living experience of the practical work of the Centre – real human lives encountering the sacred through the insights and wisdom of Celtic spirituality. It was also written as a help to the many people who want a straightforward introduction to Celtic spirituality, with an emphasis on practical living.

At this time in the world there are many people who are

'seeking' in a spiritual sense. Often at the heart of this search is a desire for a living experience of God (or 'Sacred Presence' or 'Higher Power' or whichever words people use to describe this aspect of experience) – rather than theoretical sermons and theological teaching 'about' God. There is also a desire for that living experience to be authentic, to have real depth and to speak to the needs of the heart for mystery and sacred beauty in a materialistic, post-modern age where 'reality' is reduced to the 'measurable', perceived through the lens of the scientific worldview. In addition, there is a longing for a life of real meaning and deep satisfaction that is lived ethically, authentically and with courage.

I think this is why so many find inspiration through the experience of Celtic spirituality, which has the potential to reconnect us with the Sacred Presence at the heart of life, with the rest of creation and with the beauty of our own authentic selves. Through Celtic spirituality comes a call to a deeper, more interconnected and aware way of being.

* * *

I now want to explain the approach which I intend to take in introducing Celtic spirituality and also the sequence in which the content of this book will be presented, beginning with a little bit of background to set the context.

The Background

Celtic spirituality draws its inspiration from the first Christians of the early church in Ireland – and other early Christian churches of these islands – from the early fifth century. Influences from pre-Christian Celtic civilisation combined with the rural way of life in Ireland meant that the first Christian church here was quite distinct in its development (though obviously not totally separate), and to this day much remains to remind us of our ancestors in the faith – remote monastic sites, high crosses and towers, and the wonderful artworks of the illuminated manuscripts, such as the *Book of Kells*.

At the outset I would like to say that it may be that some of the contemporary interest in Celtic Christianity is historically simplistic – looking at the past, as it were, in 'soft focus' – with a background of Celtic mists, hypnotic harps and golden sunsets! In his book *Living Between Worlds: place and journey in Celtic Spirituality*, Philip Sheldrake draws attention to the complexities of the early church in Ireland. He says, firstly, that it was multi-dimensional, with many regional variations. Secondly, that it is too simplistic to suggest that there was a totally separate 'Celtic church', unconnected to the rest of Western Christendom and 'uncontaminated' by association with the Constantinian corruption of Roman Christianity. Yes, the church in Ireland was geographically isolated, and as a scattered rural society, thought of church organisation in a quite different way from the more urbanised and settled world of Roman experience. Yes, there was a more 'flexible, relatively loose or fluid structure in Celtic Christianity' – but it was never totally separate.

However, bearing in mind the unhelpful exaggerations or simplifications of some modern interpretations of the practices of Celtic Christianity, Sheldrake also argues that there are 'spiritual values and themes' in the early Christian churches of these islands, which make Celtic Christianity and spirituality distinctive. He also suggests that in recent years 'a strong reassertion of regional identity in the British Isles' has resulted in a search for deeper roots and a deeper cultural identity. So – 'Celtic people, experiencing Christian faith within Celtic cultural contexts, exist in a continual line up to the present day.'[1]

However, this book is not saying that we all need to be 'Celtic Christians' or to belong to a 'Celtic church'; rather, that there are channels of inspiration, wisdom and encouragement which come through Celtic spirituality as an enrichment to the church today – whichever church denomination you happen to belong to – if any.

In this book I want to introduce Celtic spirituality, not with a historical, objective approach, but as a living experience, arising out of the practical work of The Centre for Celtic Spirituality, inspirational and creative for the contemporary spiritual search.

We called this ministry 'The Centre for Celtic Spirituality' instead of 'Christianity' for a particular reason – Celtic Christianity roots us in a study of a particular period of history, whereas Celtic spirituality is about drawing inspiration from the past for the contemporary spiritual journey.

For those who want a historical approach to exploring Celtic Christianity there are many books and study courses already available, some of which are recommended in the Further Resources section at the back of this book.

So in this book I will introduce six aspects of Celtic spirituality which are clearly interconnected, and which would seem to speak particularly to the age in which we are living and offer practical inspiration for the challenges and the spiritual search of our time.

They are as follows:-

1. Creation – our relationship with the rest of creation.
2. Hospitality – our relationship with ourselves and others.
3. A Way of Living – how what we believe is foundational to lifestyle.
4. Creative spirituality – relating to the spiritual with the whole of our humanity.
5. Pilgrimage – spiritual journey.
6. The Other World – death, saints and angels.

These six aspects will be explored by considering the scriptures, the life of Christ, the liturgy and practices of the early church in Ireland and other early Christian churches of these islands, and also through the sharing of present day experiences and current writings in the area of Celtic spirituality. These six elements are by no means exhaustive with regard to the riches of Celtic spirituality – there is much more that could be said and included. However, they fulfill the intention of this book's title – *Sacred Living* – because they are each to do with the practical issues and challenges of daily life – and Celtic spirituality is always more about experience than objective knowledge. So each chapter will also offer some practical questions and suggestions for further thought and action.

Each aspect also draws us to an awareness of the Sacred Presence at the heart of life – a presence which, when we become conscious of it, gives meaning and light to the whole of life.

In the coming chapters, may you find inspiration for your spiritual journey and 'a coat of many colours' in the vibrancy and variety of Celtic spirituality. Most of all, may you encounter the Sacred Presence at the heart of your life.

Blessed be the longing that brought you here
And quickens your soul with wonder.

May you have the courage to listen to the voice of desire
That disturbs you when you have settled for something safe.

May you have the wisdom to enter generously into your own unease
To discover the new direction your longing wants you to take.

May you come to accept your longing as divine urgency.

May you know the urgency with which God longs for you.[2]
(From 'For Longing' by John O'Donohue from *Benedictus*)

CHAPTER ONE

Our relationship with the rest of creation

'When I have a terrible need of – shall I say the word? – religion

...

Then I go out and paint the stars.'
– Vincent Van Gogh (1853-1890)

In 2009 I was doing some work for the Irish Peace Centres[1] and I was fascinated to discover that one of the programmes offered through the Glencree Centre for Peace and Reconciliation was a 'nature-based' experience.

Mixed groups of 'ex-combatants' – from the Paramilitaries or the various branches of the British army – were placed in a survival situation together for several weeks – sometimes in the highlands of Scotland or in wilderness areas of South Africa. These people, from very different backgrounds, who had been enemies during the years of conflict in Northern Ireland, were placed in a situation where they had to work together for their survival. Over the weeks, aspects of their common humanity were clearly revealed as they shared the highs and lows of their wilderness existence. The constant presence of Mother nature (though often 'red in tooth and claw'!) created opportunities, away from the masks of civilisation, for deep connection and real healing of relationship, though it was often a very difficult inner journey.

This illustration is only one example of many, where connection with the natural world brings opportunity for the healing of the troubled twenty-first century psyche.

Our contemporary ways of living are often completely cut off from the natural cycles of the earth and the rest of creation. Yet the soul part of ourselves longs for peace and real depth of connection in this fast-moving, technological and complex world, where many people find themselves isolated and alone.

In addition, in an age of environmental crisis, when news reports are regularly about global warming, depletion of the ozone layer, the rise of cancer, over-population, pollution, famine, increased volcanic activity and fundamental changes to the earth's environment – no wonder there is a deep anxiety about the future of the planet in the hearts of many people! A primary school teacher told me recently that some of the children in her class were having nightmares about 'the end of the world'!

In The Centre for Celtic Spirituality, many visitors and pilgrims share their longings for the possibility of a different relationship with the rest of creation – a relationship of true connection and respect. Many have looked, with a new appreciation, at the lives of indigenous peoples such as the Native American Indians, who lived 'with' the cycles of nature and with a deep respect for the other species with whom we share the earth. They already understood what the scientists have more recently 'discovered' – the importance of the eco-systems and that all species are mutually interdependent.

This holistic view of the universe is also being rediscovered today by modern physics which has demonstrated that living organisms are integrated energetic systems within an integrated universe, and because of our interconnectedness, our actions directly affect one another.

1. Celtic Christianity and nature

This deep connection and respect often practised by indigenous peoples was also present in the Celtic Christianity which perceived the Sacred Presence, not only in human beings, but in all of creation.

The early Celtic Christians lived – not just close to nature – but *with* nature. They had an overwhelming consciousness of the immanence of God within the natural world in a non-dualistic way.

The Irish monastic tradition emphasised simplicity and the wildness and solitude of the natural world. For example, the story of the Irish monk, Ciarán, whose first disciples were 'a bear, a fox, a badger, a wolf and a hind' – the inference clearly is that the natural world also has the power to 'recognise' the sacred.

In his book *The Mountain Behind the Mountain*, Noel Dermot

O'Donoghue speaks about how the Celtic mind sees the natural world as a revelation of the Divine, and a place of encounter with God.[2] Professor John Macquarrie in *Paths in Spirituality* identifies the key feature of Celtic Spirituality as 'an intense sense of presence'.[3]

St Patrick's Breastplate is a powerful example of the power of God linked with the power of nature:

> I gird myself today with the might of heaven;
> The rays of the sun, the beams of the moon,
> The glory of fire, the speed of wind,
> The depth of sea, the stability of earth,
> I gird myself today with the power of God.

All of this speaks powerfully to an age of alienation from nature and of environmental destruction, reminding us of a more holistic gospel and a world, as Gerald Manley Hopkins wrote, 'Charged with the grandeur of God'.

2. *The Bible and Creation*

Underlying all of this in Celtic spirituality is an understanding of scripture which emphasises the sacredness of creation.

Firstly, the Bible opens with the creation story in Genesis chapter one, and the point of the story – whether or not one is coming from a literal 'Creationist' perspective – is that all things come from the Divine Source, therefore all things are sacred.

In chapter one these words are repeated seven times: 'And God saw that it was good.' So the Bible begins with this picture of 'original goodness' and, although the story of 'The Fall' comes shortly afterwards, still the message of Genesis chapter one ought not to be lost – at the heart of all creation is the original goodness over which evil can never ultimately triumph.

Secondly, the coming of Christ is not only about the salvation of human beings, as Romans 8 makes clear: 'The creation itself will be set free from its bondage to decay and will obtain the freedom of the glory of the children of God' (See Romans 8:18-22). The message of the incarnation is a fusing of the Spirit and the material – God becoming one of us – so the dualistic perspective that divides up the material (sinful) and the spiritual (holy) is challenged by incarnation.

Thirdly, all of creation is sacramental because the visible creation is a reminder of the invisible presence of God – not in a Pantheistic sense, where God is synonymous with the material – but in a Panentheistic sense – God is *in* all creation, but also timelessly extends beyond creation. So, for example, the psalmist described this aspect of experience – seeing the Divine Presence in the creation – in Psalm 19: 'The heavens are telling the glory of God; and the firmament proclaims his handiwork. Day to day pours forth speech, and night to night declares knowledge.'

3. Inspirations for contemporary living

Out of all of this come a multitude of implications for how we understand our connection and live in relationship with the rest of creation.

For example, if Creation is sacramental then we need to acknowledge that understanding in our personal daily life choices and in our choices as a society in terms of our consumption of the earth's resources. From the perspective of the western business world, all of us are 'consumers' and the more we can be encouraged to consume the better, from their point of view. Yet any relationship which is all 'take, take, take' is not sustainable. I read words recently which were spoken by the Cree Native Americans as a prophecy, which said:

> Only after the last tree has been cut down,
> Only after the last river has been poisoned,
> Only after the last fish has been caught,
> Only then will you realise that money cannot be eaten.

As a society, and as individuals, we need to find ways of living more simply and of giving back to the earth, with gratitude and with blessing.

This simplicity of living and deep respect for creation was at the heart of the practice and the liturgies of Celtic Christianity, and inspiration from such sources can be a powerful well of blessing for the contemporary spiritual path. J. Philip Newell, former warden of Iona Abbey, was telling us at a recent conference in Armagh about the way in which pilgrims to Iona value going for prayer and meditation to the ruins of the old convent there, with the roof open to the sky, in preference to the en-

CHAPTER ONE   19

closed spaces of the solid Abbey building. Celtic Christians often worshipped out of doors, gathered around the high crosses or at the holy wells.

At The Centre for Celtic Spirituality we have a practice of taking groups regularly to the old local well dedicated to St Brigid, and praying for healing using water from the well. If creation is sacramental, then the potential for encountering the Sacred Presence in the natural world is powerful. Many people find healing experiences in connection with nature and there are also a myriad of possibilities for approaching prayer and worship.

For example, when I served as curate assistant of the parish of Newtownards, County Down, they had a wonderful practice each year of pilgrimaging together on the Sunday nearest to St Columba's Day to the ruins of an old Abbey, where Holy Communion was celebrated under the open sky. It was always a very special occasion and connected the people with their own history of faith in that local community.

To perceive the creation as sacramental is to experience the Sacred Presence in every aspect of the natural world – not just the beauty of the spring and summer and the bounty of harvest, but also the dark and cold days of the winter season which brings death and decay and reminds us of the cycles of death and new life. It is also to experience the fulfillment of the first chapter of John's gospel, 'The Word became flesh and lived among us.'

There is an ancient Irish poem which sees the Sacred Presence in all of creation in these wonderful words:

I am the wind that breathes upon the sea,
I am the wave on the ocean,
I am the murmur of leaves rustling,
I am the rays of the sun,
I am the beam of the moon and stars,
I am the power of trees growing,
I am the bud breaking into blossom,
I am the movement of the salmon swimming,
I am the courage of the wild boar fighting,
I am the speed of the stage running,
I am the strength of the ox pulling the plough,

I am the size of the mighty oak tree,
And I am the thoughts of all people
Who praise my beauty and grace.[4]

Creation: Practical Inspirations

Individual

1. Look at your own daily life choices. Are there ways you
   could live more simply or practice the ethic of respect for the
   rest of creation more clearly?
2. In your daily life, consciously absorb the beauty of the natural
   world, and let it be a source of joy and peace.
3. Make a prayer space for yourself out of doors. Perhaps under
   a tree or somewhere where you can receive from the sacra
   ment of nature.
4. Support organisations which care for the earth or animal
   welfare beyond the commercial interests of consumerism
   and big business.

Community

1. Find ways of connecting with the natural world in prayer
   groups or walking pilgrimages.
2. Be a voice in your local community for the preservation of
   green spaces.
3. Support organisations which care for the environment in
   your annual allocations as well as 'human-centred' work.
   Invite someone from Friends of the Earth or another envi
   ronmental organisation to address a church group or a
   Sunday service, e.g. harvest thanksgiving.
4. Become an Eco-congregation. For ideas see www.ecocongre
   gation.org

CHAPTER TWO

Hospitality: Caring for the soul

'People don't care how much you know,
until they know how much you care.'
– *Attributed to Theodore Roosevelt*

Celtic Christianity's emphasis on hospitality as a way of life is, I
believe, one of the most inspirational aspects of Celtic spirituality
for the spiritual search of our day, because it offers sanctuary for
the soul and acknowledges, with respect, the fragile nature of
the spiritual search.

1. Celtic Christianity and Hospitality
In the Celtic tradition there are countless stories of the generosity
of the Celtic saints, such as St Brigid, who from her earliest days
had the practice of giving all she could to the poor.

The Celtic monastic communities were not only places of
prayer and learning – they were also places of sanctuary and
hospitality. It is said that before he went to Iona, St Columba's
monastery in Derry fed up to 1,000 callers every day!

At Glendalough, to this day, can be seen the infirmary where
the women were treated, tranquilly situated a little way from
the main tourist track.

This practice of 'holistic' hospitality was rooted in the teaching of the early church, based on Hebrews 13:2: 'Do not neglect
to show hospitality to strangers, for by doing so some have en-
tertained angels unawares.' Their hospitality was scripturally
based and placed a high value on the sacredness of the individual soul.

In his wonderful book, *Christ of the Celts*, J. Philip Newell
speaks of this sacredness envisioned in the first chapters of
Genesis, when male and female are created 'in the image of
God' (Genesis 1:27). He says:

A nineteenth century teacher in the Celtic world, Alexander Scott, used the analogy of royal garments. Apparently in his day, royal garments were woven through with a costly thread, a thread of gold. And if somehow the golden thread were taken out of the garment, the whole garment would unravel. So it is, he said, with the image of God woven into the fabric of our being. If it were taken out of us we would unravel. We would cease to be. So the image of God is not simply a characteristic of who we are, which may or may not be there depending on whether or not we have been baptised. The image of God is the essence of our being. It is the core of our human soul. We are sacred not because we have been baptized or because we belong to one faith tradition over another. We are sacred because we have been born.[1]

There is a wonderful story from the fifth century about St Martin of Tours who, whilst out riding on his horse one day, passed a naked beggar on the road. He had such compassion for the man that he removed the cloak he was wearing and gave it to the beggar. That night he had a dream in which Christ appeared to him, wearing the very cloak he had given to the beggar that day. And Christ spoke to him and said: 'Whatever you do, to the least of these your brothers and sisters, you do to me' (Matthew 25:40).

This was the vision that was at the heart of the hospitality practiced by Celtic Christianity – seeing the Christ in every person.

2. The Practice of Hospitality today
The implications for how we encounter one another – and, indeed, how we treat ourselves – are many.

(a) The Open Heart
Firstly, hospitality calls us to be open, non-judgmental, generous and gentle in our attitudes to ourselves and to one another, recognising the sacredness of the soul.

By its nature, the spiritual search is a fragile one and the seeking soul needs to be treated with care and with respect – we only see the outward appearance, but God sees the heart

(1 Samuel 16:7).

There's a lovely story told by Anthony De Mello in *The Heart of the Enlightened* about a little girl who had been told that Lincoln wasn't very good-looking and she was taken to see the President at the White House. Lincoln took her on his knees and chatted with her for a while in his gentle, humorous way. Suddenly the little girl called out, 'Daddy! He isn't ugly at all. He's just beautiful!'[2]

The point of the story is to have the wisdom and the grace to see beyond the external to the beauty of the human soul.

(b) The Fragile Soul

Secondly, there are implications for how we offer welcome and a safe space to wounded souls seeking pastoral care.

I heard recently about a Roman Catholic priest in New York who was concerned about the numbers of people who were leaving the worshipping community of his church and decided to initiate a café-style discussion group, open to all. He thought he would discover a lot of people with various arguments and reasons as to why they could no longer believe in Christian doctrine and theology. Instead what he encountered were many people who no longer felt welcome in the church community – people who carried personal hurts and wounds and felt they could not truly be themselves and be accepted in the church.

To offer hospitality in the pattern of the early church in Ireland means that we need first of all just to be willing to listen. Listening is foundational.

For example, over the past few years my husband and I have been fostering children. Often small children when they're first taken into care are unable to express their needs – they sit still and silent, totally different from the usual children of their age. This is because they are totally unused to anyone listening to their requests. The severe neglect they've suffered brings with it a total silence. In their new home they have to begin to learn that someone actually cares enough to listen to them. The healing of the child begins with the adult who cares enough to listen.

By listening, we give another soul its dignity. By refusing to listen (and this applies even if we think we will disagree with the person we're listening to) we're relegating the person to anonymity and disrespecting the sacredness of the soul. For example, read the encounter of Jesus and the woman at the well of Samaria in John chapter 4 – Jesus may not have agreed with everything about the Samaritan woman, but he truly listened to her heart.

Hospitality begins with an open and listening heart.

Ultimately to offer hospitality as exemplified by Celtic Christianity – in open and non-judgemental welcome – is to mirror the unconditional love of God shown to us in Jesus Christ.

(c) The Healing of the Self

Thirdly, there are implications for how we perceive ourselves. When Jesus said 'Love your neighbour as yourself''', he made a connection between love of oneself and love of others. The reality is – and this is also borne out by modern psychology – that if we have no self-respect, it is difficult, if not impossible, to offer hospitality to others. We need to understand and value our own sacredness.

A Personal story

Some years ago I had a dream which transformed my understanding of the soul's sacredness.

In the dream I was walking down wide, stone steps, leading into a huge pyramid structure. At the bottom of the steps dust and sand covered the floor and I took up a broom and began to sweep. As I swept away the layers of sand and dust, gradually – and to my complete joy – a beautiful, colourful, mosaic-tiled floor began to be uncovered. Its symmetry and glorious colour were breathtaking. The experience of the dream was one of sheer joy, healing and bliss. I awoke with all of the joy and peace still within me, and remained still for a long time, absorbing the beauty of the dream and wondering about its meaning.

To me it seemed clear that the mosaic floor represented the beauty of the soul. Through life's experiences that beauty may get covered over with the dust and the dirt of living. Yet the beauty of our soul remains intact, no matter what life throws at us, to be uncovered and revealed as we realise our own sacredness and learn to value ourselves.

This dream revealed to me that ultimately our potential for healing is within our own souls. Externals such as possessions, money, jobs, holidays, houses – even other people – cannot bring the healing peace we long for. True hospitality begins with listening to one's own soul – charity (love) begins at home.

The western world has become disconnected from the soul at the heart of life. In his book *Care of the Soul*, Thomas Moore speaks of the need to nurture and value our neglected souls in order to find the way to wholeness and deep joy in living. He says, 'The great malady of the twentieth century, implicated in all of our troubles and affecting us individually and socially, is "loss of soul". When soul is neglected it doesn't just go away; it appears symptomatically in obsessions, addictions, violence and loss of meaning. Our temptation is to isolate these symptoms or to try to eradicate them one by one; but the root problem is that we have lost our wisdom about the soul, even our interest in it.'[3]

The hospitality practised by the early church in Ireland opens up for us an ancient well of wisdom and inspiration for our soulless age. It calls us, firstly, to practise hospitality and caring for our own soul, recognising our own sacred value and beauty. Then to relate to others with that same spirit of hospitality, in openness, gentleness and generosity, respecting the soul, made in the image of God.

There is a lovely Celtic rune of hospitality used by the Iona Community which says:

I saw a stranger last night.
I put food in the eating place,
Drink in the drinking place,
Music in the listening place,
And in the Name of the Triune God,
He blessed myself and my cattle and my dear ones.
And the lark said in her song,
'Often, often, often, goes the Christ in the stranger's guise.'

Hospitality: Practical inspirations

Individual

1. In what ways do you perceive and value the beauty of your
    own soul? Are you gentle and forgiving with yourself, or do
    you batter yourself with feelings of guilt and inadequacy?
    The author Louise Hay recommends this as a daily exercise
    (she says many find it very difficult initially but with practice
    it brings healing): Look at yourself in a mirror. Look into
    your own eyes. See yourself, without judgement. Have com
    passion for yourself. Welcome yourself, with words of love.
2. Find ways of recovering your soul – make time in your life
    for wells of creativity – reflection, prayer / meditation, ab
    sorbing beauty, reading, art, walking in nature.
3. Practise listening from the heart. Hospitality welcomes 'the
    stranger' – be honest; who is the stranger for you? Perhaps
    someone from another church or faith community, a gay or
    lesbian person, a 'foreigner', someone in prison? Most of us
    hold some prejudices, but it helps to be aware of our pre-
    judging attitudes, and be open to listening.

Community

1. Re-evaluate your 'welcome' strategies for your church com
    munity. In what ways are strangers made to feel welcome?
    In what ways can we improve our welcome to all?
2. Move beyond the 'holy huddle' model of church. Become an
    outward looking community, inspired to be a channel of
    practical hospitality to the wider community – assess and re
    spond to the needs in your particular area.
3. Be open to working together with other churches, other faith
    communities in your area. Pooling resources can bring
    greater possibilities and opportunities for new initiatives.

CHAPTER THREE

A way of living

'I don't believe people are looking for the meaning of life
as much as they are looking for the experience of being alive.'
– *Joseph Campbell*

A few miles from the peninsula town of Newtownards in County Down in the North of Ireland, is the fifth century monastic site of Nendrum. Situated on Mahee Island, accessible by a bridge road, it is a place of beauty and tranquility, where the ancient stones reveal three enclosures: a ruined church and graves, a sundial and a round tower.

During the years when I served a curacy in the parish of Newtownards, I often went to Nendrum – to pray and to be inspired by the way of living represented by this ancient place.

At the heart of this community was the church, the sundial and the graveyard (representing prayer and the sacredness of time, from birth to death). The second enclosure contained a monastic school and workshops for making necessary vessels and tools. The outer enclosure was for animals and food growing. In more recent years archaeologists have also discovered sea water 'tide-mills' at Nendrum, dating from the seventh century – the oldest known preserved tide-mills in the world.

We are so fortunate in Ireland to have these ancient places to remind us of a sacred way of living – a 'holistic' way of life that prioritised the sacredness of the soul.

The early church in Ireland, because of the rural way of life (in contrast to the big urban cities where the disciples first preached the gospel), was quite distinct in its development and organisation. Also, because Ireland was never part of the Roman Empire, early Irish Christianity was always a little distant from the mainstream of the institution. Greek philosophy and Roman law were very important to the central church, but neither had taken deep root in Ireland. Celtic Christianity's approach to Sacred Living was more rooted in the cycles of the natural world and 'native' spirituality tended to work more out of a theology of immanence, rather than transcendence. Influenced by the desert fathers and mothers, the early church in Ireland had a tradition of community living and also of isolated hermits. A wonderful example is Glendalough in the mountains of County Wicklow, where the remains of community living can be seen to this day, in addition to the remote cells of hermit monks, such as St Kevin.

There are three particular aspects of this sacred way of living that I believe are inspirational for the spiritual search of our time.

1. The sacredness of time

The underlying assumption for this sacred way of living was that all of life was full of the Divine Presence – God immanent in the world of time – and all time was sacred.

(a) Non-Dualistic

Sometimes in our understanding of time, we have a tendency to divide up life into 'sacred/profane' and have a very elevated view of the 'holy' over the ordinary, whereas Celtic spirituality reminds us that there is no division between the sacred and the secular – all of life is sacred , lived in the Presence of God.

I remember some years ago a lady came up to me after I had celebrated the sacrament of Holy Communion and said: 'I'm sure you wonder why I didn't come forward to receive Holy Communion? It's because I'm going to a dance later on.'

She had in her mind a division between the sacred (Holy Communion) and the profane (the dancing), and felt it would be wrong to mix the two, whereas Celtic spirituality perceives the sacred in all of life. As John O'Donohue said in *Anamchara*, 'The Celtic mind was not burdened by dualism. It did not separate what belongs together ... the dualism which separates the visible from the invisible, time from eternity, the human from the divine, was totally alien to them.'[1]

This sense of all of time infused with the Sacred Presence is spoken of in the scriptures. Psalm 113:3 says, 'From the rising of the sun to its setting, the name of the Lord is to be praised.' So, from fire-lighting in the morning to the setting of the sun in the evening, every part of an ordinary day was sacred.

An ancient prayer in the Celtic tradition called *Kindling the Fire* echoes this approach to life:

> This morning, as I kindle the fire upon my hearth, I pray that the flame of God's love may burn in my heart, and the hearts of all I meet today.
>
> I pray that no envy and malice, no hatred or fear, may smother the flame.
>
> I pray that indifference and apathy, contempt and pride, may not pour like cold water on the fire.
>
> Instead, may the spark of God's love light the love in my heart, that it may burn brightly through the day.
>
> And may I warm those that are lonely, whose hearts are cold and lifeless, so that all may know the comfort of God's love.[2]

We may not be much involved these days in the lighting of fires in the morning (or at any other time!), but to be conscious of the Sacred Presence in each moment of our ordinary day brings significance and meaning to the whole of life.

(b) The Concept of 'Neart'

In his fascinating book, *Where Three Streams Meet*, Seán Ó Duinn talks about influences which came through the pre-Christian traditions into the early church in Ireland. One of these was the concept of *Neart*. It is the understanding that there is a 'transcendent reality pervading all things in the world … a divine presence filling everything …' In him we live and move and have our being.[3]

This perception of the 'Soul' in everything, reminds me of a poem by Dylan Thomas from the Welsh tradition which says:

> The force that through the green fuse drives the flower
> drives my green age …
> The force that drives the water through the rocks
> Drives my red blood …

It is a vision of a power at the heart of everything that links us all and permeates all. Ó Duinn says 'God in this his creative energy or *'neart'* is seen as going out in six directions … He surrounds the person on all sides: north, south, east, west, above and below.'

So this concept of the six directions is expressed in the Lorica of St Brendan, and Ó Duinn quotes as follows:

Críost romham (Christ before me);
Críost ar mo dheis (Christ at my right hand);
Críost i mo dhiaidh (Christ behind me);
Críost ar mo chlé (Christ at my left hand);
Críost os mo chionn (Christ above me);
Críost fúm (Christ below me).[4]

To perceive '*neart*' is to experience the power of the Sacred Presence, 'the Soul' in all of life.

(c) Calendar and Sacred Ritual

In his lecture series in All Hallows, Dublin, Fr John Joe Spring, Vice President of All Hallows, drawing on Ó Duinn and others, spoke about the pre-Christian Celtic understanding of the cycle of the year – the sacred calendar – which also influenced Celtic Christianity. The ancient Celts observed four particular seasons.

Firstly, *Samhain* (November to January), the winter quarter. The year begins in cold and darkness, a time traditionally associated with the remembrance of the ancestors, when the veil between this world and the next is thin (a 'thin' time).
Secondly, *Imbolc* (February to April), the spring quarter, which marked the resurrection of new life in the natural world.
Thirdly, *Bealtaine* (May to July), when confidence and vitality were celebrated in summer festivals.
Fourthly, *Lughnasa* (August to October), the time of maturity, gathering and the harvest of the land.

Christianity in Ireland celebrated its festivals, drawing on these ancient perspectives of the sacred calendar. For example, *Samhain* became All Saints/All Souls, when those who have gone before us to the next life are remembered with thanksgiving. At the darkest time of the year – Winter solstice – the Celts marked the rebirth of the sun in places like Newgrange. Christians celebrate the birth of the Son of God, the light of the world. During *Imbolc* Christians now celebrate Easter – the festival of the resurrection of Christ to new life.

To live in harmony with the cycles of nature and to perceive their sacred significance through ritual is to practice the sanctification of time. From this perspective life is not meaningless and empty, but a daily blessing, lived with awareness and joy.

In his book *Benedictus*, John O'Donohue laments the loss of ritual in 21st century living. He says that the loss of ritual leaves us naked in our rites of passage:

> Our culture has little to offer us for our crossings. Never was there such talk of communication or such technology to facilitate it. Yet at the heart of our new-found wealth and progress there is a gaping emptiness and we are haunted by loneliness ... With the demise of religion, many people are left stranded in a chasm of emptiness and doubt; without rituals to recognise, celebrate or negotiate the vital thresholds of their lives, the key crossings pass by, undistinguished from the mundane, everyday rituals of life ... If we approach our decisive thresholds with reverence and attention, the crossing will bring us more than we could ever have hoped for ... In our present ritual poverty, the Celtic tradition has much to offer us.[5]

2. Anamchara

Another inspirational aspect of Celtic Christianity's way of living was the practice of Anamchara.

Anam is the Gaelic word for soul, and *cara* is the word for friend. So Anamchara literally means 'soul-friend' or 'the friend of the soul.'

Perhaps based on the practice of Jesus who sent out his disciples two by two, each Christian had a soul friend, a wise advisor, who would listen, pray and share wisdom. In his book *The Celtic Way*, Ian Bradley explains:

> They combined the roles of spiritual director, guru, confessor and confidential counsellor. For the monks they were of particular importance – many abbots acknowledged that it was more important to follow one's soul friend than to obey the monastic rules – but they were also much used by the laity. One of the most famous sayings from the Celtic Christian world, attributed variously to St Comgall, St Brigid and others, is that a person without a soul friend is like a body without a head.[6]

In his beautiful book *Anamchara*, John O'Donohue explores
in depth the value and meaning of the soul friend for our contemporary age. He says,

> The anamchara was a person to whom you could reveal the hid-
> den intimacies of your life. This friendship was an act of recog-
> nition and belonging. When you had an anamchara, your
> friendship cut across all convention and category. You were
> joined in an ancient and eternal way with the friend of your
> soul.[7]

In small ways the wisdom of this ancient practice is now
being rediscovered through what is called 'spiritual direction.'
Ian Bradley comments:

> Modern experts in the field of spiritual counselling and clinical
> psychology are coming to see the advantages of this Celtic model
> of pastoral care which faced up to the need we all have for regu-
> larly unburdening our souls without having to resort to the for-
> mal ritual of the guilt-inducing aspects of the confessional.[8]

Perhaps a full recovery of this ancient practice of Anamchara
in the life of the church would provide support for clergy (who
often serve in unbelievable isolation) and prevent the pastoral
crises that have occurred too often in recent years?

3. Justice
A third inspirational aspect of the Celtic Christianity's 'Way of
Living' was the practice of justice in its structures. Because of
the isolation and rural, tribal nature of Ireland, the Irish church,
instead of administering through diocesan organisation – the
hierarchical pattern of the central church – organised itself in
small community life.

Church personnel, such as bishops or priests, weren't as oc-
cupied with administrative functions, and so theirs could be a
spiritual ministry that was not necessarily tied to a fixed location. In the Celtic monasteries there were both married and celi-
bate monks, and women as well as men took monastic vows.
There was no uniform liturgy, hymn book, episcopal authority,
central strategy, or central funding (some might say, 'thank God
for progress!').

There is also evidence of more gender equality and less patriarchy, especially evident in figures like St Brigid of Kildare, St Ita of Killeedy and St Hilda of Whitby, who presided over the Council of Whitby in AD 664. When a missionary was needed in one place, help was simply requested from another community. Practice was varied; there was no central organisation, yet the church was held together by their relationship to God in Christ, by the power of the Holy Spirit – Trinitarian unity, the true nature of a catholic church.

The focus of the early church in Ireland on justice in relationships and structures is an inspiration to the church today and reflects the words of Isaiah, which inspired the ministry of Jesus: 'To bring good news to the poor, to proclaim release to the captives, to let the oppressed go free ...' (Luke 4:18).

4. Simplicity

The way of living practised by the monks of the Celtic Christian community varied between prayer, study, teaching and physical work. It was a sustainable way of living which practised a simplicity of life and at its heart had a concern for the poor. Churches were usually constructed of wood, and rarely expensively decorated. If a church became too small for their needs or fell into disrepair, then another would be built. Instead of focusing on buildings, their focus was on people, and money was used to obtain freedom for slaves and to feed the poor.

A poem attributed to St Columba gives us an interesting picture of this Way of Living, inspired by the blessings of creation, which combines worship, study, work, charitable deeds and contemplation:

That I might bless the Lord
Who orders all;
Heaven with its countless bright orders,
Land, strand and flood,
That I might search in all the books
That would help my soul;
At times kneeling to the heaven of my heart, at times singing psalms;
At times contemplating the King of Heaven,

Chief of the Holy Ones;
At times at work without compulsion,
This would be delightful.
At times plucking duilisc from the rocks
At other times fishing
At times distributing food to the poor
At times in a hermitage.[9]

All of this reflects the poverty and simplicity of the life of Jesus, who from his humble birth through his life as a wandering preacher and teacher, to his death – buried in the tomb of another – was an example of humility and simplicity.

Jesus said, 'It is easier for a camel to go through the eye of a needle than for someone who is rich to enter the kingdom of God' (Matthew 19:24) and 'You cannot serve God and wealth' (Matthew 6:24). This is because 'Where your treasure is, there your heart will be also' (Matthew 6:21).

Down the centuries many have been inspired by the simplicity of the life of Christ and have felt called to renounce material luxuries in order to be true disciples. People like St Francis of Assisi, who chose a life of poverty, the Celtic hermits, and many of the monastic orders, whose vows often include a 'vow of poverty'.

The simplicity of this way of living as it was practised by the early church in Ireland is an inspiration to our age which is obsessed with material possessions as the source of satisfaction. Yet many live in grinding poverty while others accumulate far more than they will ever need in this lifetime. As a result there are huge challenges to the world's resources as the human population increases (forecast to be 9 billion by 2050) and we urgently need to seek sustainable ways of living in harmony and with respect for the rest of creation.

Christian Aid have challenged us with their slogan – 'Live simply, so that others may simply live' – and that also includes the rest of God's creation at a time when species extinction is rapidly increasing due to erosion of habitats.

There is so much more that could be said about this aspect of Celtic Christianity's way of living, and further resources are included at the end of this book. Ultimately all we have comes from the Great Giver and is only ours on a temporary loan. As someone replied, when asked at a funeral 'How much did he leave?' – 'Everything …'

A Way of Living: Practical Inspirations

Individual

1. Establish a daily practice of giving thanks for the blessings of the day – the sanctification of time. Write a 'gratitude' journal.
2. Seek an anamchara – someone whose wise advice will be a source of encouragement and nurturing for your soul.
3. Examine your life – in what ways could you clear space / de-clutter / live more simply? See *The Thrift Book* by India Knight (Penguin 2008)

Community

1. Find new festivals that truly connect with peoples' lives. For example, a service of remembrance at All Saints' Tide, in which the names of all who have died over the past year are read out and to which all families bereaved over the past year (or two years) are invited.

   In reformed churches in particular the dead are rarely spoken of. Those churches who have initiated this annual service have found that it attracts large numbers of people, proving the need which people have to continue in relation ship with their loved ones who have gone to the next life.
2. If your church building is closed during the week, consider opening it up, so that anyone passing by can pray in the sa cred space. Offer prayer suggestions and even sources of help and counselling for those in need.
3. Continually reconsider the vision and priorities of your group or church in terms of your local area. Are you relevant to the needs in your area? Consider the words of Jesus in Luke chapter 4. Have a vision day for the church and / or a fo cused retreat for the church or group leaders.
4. Are there ways in which you could practice simplicity as a group / church? Perhaps recycling, saving energy or using fairly-traded products.

CHAPTER FOUR

Creative spirituality:
Relating to the spiritual with the whole of our humanity

'It is the creative potential itself in human beings
that is the image of God.'
– *Mary Daly*

On a hot summer's afternoon in Trinity College, Dublin, the queue of people waiting to see the *Book of Kells* is never-ending. Well over 1000 years old, the *Book of Kells* (*Leabhar Cheanannais*), also known as the Book of Columba or the Book of Colum Cille, includes the four gospels of the New Testament, written in Latin in beautiful calligraphic art and decorated with all sorts of illuminations and images in vibrant colours.

Watching all those people – visitors from many different countries in the world – I wonder to myself, 'What is it that draws their interest to this ancient manuscript, created in the early seventh century? Why have the images from the *Book of Kells* resonated with the imaginations and souls of all nationalities over hundreds of years? What has the early church in Ireland to teach us today about creative spirituality?'

1. Celtic Christianity and Creative spirituality
In the early church in Ireland it is clear that a high priority was given to the realm of the Arts. This practice could have been influenced by pre-Christian Celtic society which gave the *seanachie* (storyteller), and the bard and poet equal social status to the king (political power) and the druid (spiritual power).

In *The Celtic Way* Ian Bradley says: 'The Celtic monasteries were not just religious institutions in the narrow sense. They opened their doors to seekers and scholars of all kinds and became important centres of learning and culture. In this respect they took over the role which had been fulfilled by communities of bards and *filid* in pre-Christian times ... If the monks had a scriptural inspiration for their work, it was surely Paul's injunction to the Philippians to hold unto whatsoever things are pure and lovely and good. This meant keeping alive native traditions of poetry and folksong as well as copying the scriptures, practising the art of manuscript illumination, studying classical authors, both for their philosophy and their theology and fashioning exquisite brooches and rings.[1]

There is no doubt that it is the colourful images of Celtic creativity that have attracted many to explore Celtic heritage and Celtic Christianity more fully. From the mysterious pre-Christian spiral symbols in places like Tara and Newgrange, to the majestic stonework of the Celtic Christian high crosses which still stand in the centres of many Irish towns and villages, to the sophisticated and intricate artwork and craftsmanship of the early church's monastic communities in Ireland. Monks carefully copied the gospels, embellishing them with fantastic ornamentation – spiral markings, knots, animal and human heads, plants and birds, all drawn in vivid colours.

Iconic examples of this period include, not only the *Book of Kells*, but also the *Book of Durrow* (c. 650); metalwork such as the Ardagh chalice and the Derrynaflan chalice; processional crosses such as the Tully Lough cross and the cross of Cong, and the Tara brooch.

The high crosses with the stories of the Bible carved into the stone, were a wonderful visual means of telling the story of the Christian gospel in an age when people did not either read or write. In the Armagh area we are lucky to have several Celtic high crosses – a particularly good example stands in the centre of the small village of Donaghmore, showing scenes from the life of Christ, from his birth to his resurrection. To worship like this, at the foot of the high cross, under the open sky, must have been a wonderful experience. In her book *World Made Whole: Rediscovering the Celtic Tradition*, Esther De Waal says that 'the traditional Celtic cross superimposes the cross of redemption upon the circle of the world.'[2] So that in the Celtic cross we have a visual symbol of incarnation and redemption – the world and the cross.

This creative spirituality so evident in Celtic Christianity also has roots in biblical tradition.

2. The Bible and Creativity

Genesis chapter one opens with these words: 'In the beginning God created ...' This opening picture of God is as supreme Creator/Artist.

In her wonderful book *The Artist's Way* Julia Cameron says that creativity is the essential nature of God. She goes on to say that in expressing our creativity as human beings we are aligning ourselves with the 'Creative Power' of the universe:

> If you think of the universe as a vast electrical sea in which you are immersed and from which you are formed, opening to your creativity changes you from something bobbing in that sea to a more fully functioning, more conscious, more co-operative part of that ecosystem.[3]

The feminist theologian and philosopher, Mary Daly, said: 'It is the creative potential itself in human beings that is the image of God.'

In the Old Testament book of Exodus, the craftsmen tasked with the construction of the Tabernacle – God's dwelling place – were specially blessed for their work: 'The Lord has called by name Bezalel ... and filled him with Divine Spirit, with skill, intelligence and knowledge in every kind of craft ...' (See Exodus 35:30-35).

There are the beautiful words of the psalms which were sung to the music of a variety of instruments (Psalm 150), the story of David, who 'danced before the Lord with all his might' (2 Samuel 6:14) and Jesus himself – the son of Joseph the Carpenter, in whose workshop it is assumed Jesus spent his childhood learning the skills of carpentry. Even in the last book of the Bible – the Book of Revelation – the glories of heaven are described in wonderfully creative and artistic beauty (Revelation chapter 21). It seems that creativity runs through the whole of the Bible as a sign of the gifts of the Divine Spirit working within the lives of people.

3. Modern psychology and the creative arts

Modern psychology has much to say to us about the importance of the creative impulse for human understanding and development.

For example, psychologists studying the brain have discovered that the human brain has 'right' and 'left' activity centres. The right brain is visual and processes information in an intuitive way, looking first at the whole picture and then the details. The left brain is verbal, led by logic and processes information in an analytical and sequential way, looking first at the pieces and then the whole. Both are equally vital parts of our human intelligence.

Drawing inspiration from Celtic Christian monasticism, which placed equal value on academic study, physical work and artwork, it would be a fulfilment of our humanity to achieve a balance between the right and left brain in all aspects of our lives. Imagination, creativity, intuition, spirituality and the arts could be regarded as equally important in the development of epistemology as logic, mathematics, and science. At present empiricism and the scientific worldview dominate the picture, and other ways of discerning understanding, including spirituality, are often designated as unverifiable 'myth'.

Our twenty-first century society has given the academic and the scientific worldview prime importance (for example, in the allocation of government spending) and the contribution of the creative arts is often relegated (along with spirituality) to the bottom of the league. Unfortunately this has, at times, created an artificial 'gap' between the perspectives of the arts/spirituality and science. In the last analysis, of course, truth is one, and so the deepest perspectives of spirituality and the arts ultimately complement the deepest truths of science. This can also be seen in the work of C. J. Jung regarding the human unconscious.

It may be that many people are attracted to the ancient artwork of Celtic monasticism because it appeals to something fundamental in the human subconscious. The psychologist, Carl Jung, spoke about the 'archetypes' of the human unconscious. These ancient images come to us, especially in our dreams and unconscious states, from the universal 'pool' of the human collective unconscious and connect us to one another over thousands of years. Today people are drawn to ancient mythology and prehistoric and indigenous artwork – for example, the twin spirals carved on the rocks at Newgrange – because they appeal to something much deeper than the analytical mind. The writer and mythologist, Joseph Campbell, who also explored the power of archetypes and universal symbols, said: 'Myths are public dreams; dreams are private myths.'

These insights of modern psychology underline the importance of creativity and the arts in human experience. Ultimately the creative potential within us all is a powerful source of spiritual healing.

For example, Art Therapy draws on the insights of Jung and others to offer therapeutic help through the creative process of art-making. From this perspective, creativity through art-making is seen to offer opportunities to express imagination and authenticity which can lead to emotional healing. It is often used to help disturbed children who, through the colours they choose and the images they draw, are able to communicate their deepest feelings – impossible to express verbally – and enhance their healing process. In the same way music therapy uses the emotional and ascetic aspects of music to stimulate inner healing.

These reflections on the power of creativity and the importance of art in connection with psychology and healing are inspirations from Celtic spirituality which are directly relevant to contemporary spirituality.

4. Inspirations for us today
To return to the *Book of Kells* with which we began this chapter, it has to be said that the experience of seeing the *Book of Kells* in its current setting – filing past the glass case in which it is preserved – could also be a disappointment. For example, how much more interesting it could be if the *Book of Kells* was housed in a contemporary Christian Community (preferably in Kells, or indeed Iona, where it is said to have been written), where one could gaze upon the beauty of its artwork and then be further inspired by seeing living contemporary examples of Christian art, in progress, arising out of the spirituality and creativity of the Christian faith today? This would also resonate with the essence of Celtic spirituality, which is always much more about experiences of living than theories about life.

It draws us to ask, what place is there for the practice of creativity and art in contemporary spirituality?

For example, in theological training the emphasis is almost

completely on academic research and on left-brain activity. In what ways could the artistic aspect of spirituality – so obvious in Celtic Christianity – be encouraged? It is clear that visual art often speaks more clearly to the human imagination than the written word in books or even the spoken word in sermons. So where is the place of art and creativity in theological training?

Secondly, in worship, again the emphasis can often be on books and sermons. If worship is to be a fully human activity, then it will speak to all of our human faculties – our five senses, our intuition, our creative imagination. In what ways can we smell, see, hear, taste and touch the Divine Presence?

In his recent book *At Heaven's Gate*, Richard Giles speaks about 'worship space of sensational beauty, powerful signs and symbols that can be touched and handled as well as seen ... music expertly played on appropriate instruments ... movement and drama ... interspersed with moments of total silence and awe.'[4]

Speaking personally I value worship which gives space for silence and for the mystery – something which art does so much better than black and white words – because it enables expression of the passive (waiting/listening for God) and the intuitive (discerning the Sacred Presence).

When I walk in the Mourne Mountains I admire the beauty of the skillfully built stone walls, through which the strong winds are able to blow because there are gaps between the round boulders used to create the walls. If the walls were too solid they would eventually collapse under the pressure of the high winds – the spaces are what makes for their endurance. In the same way a too 'black-and-white' theology is like a solid stone wall which leaves little room for the mystery and the flexibility that is essential for a life that is open to learning and to pilgrimage.

The creative imagination is what opens up the spaces for an intuitive seeking after God, which is at the heart of the spiritual journey.

Such creative imagination was evident in the life of the early church in Ireland and speaks to us down the centuries today, calling us to reconnect with the Creative Power at the heart of the universe, in whose image we are made.

This beautiful prayer/poem comes from the hermit tradition

of Celtic Christianity and expresses the contrast – and yet also the balance – between the left and right brain beautifully. The blackbird intuitively experiences the Sacred Presence from the heart of its being while the hermit works hard at it, intellectually.

The Hermit and the Blackbird
I need to watch the sun, to calculate the hours that I should pray to God.
But the blackbird who nests in the roof of my hut makes no such calculation:
He sings God's praises all day long.

I need books to read, to learn the hidden truths of God.
But the blackbird who shares my simple meals, needs no written texts:
He can read the love of God in every leaf and flower.

I need to beg forgiveness, to make myself pure and fit for God.
But the blackbird who drinks with me from the stream sheds no tears of contrition:
He is as God made him, with no stain of sin.

Creative Spirituality: Practical Inspirations

Individual
1. Look back at your childhood. What creative occupations did you most enjoy? For example, drawing, painting, making things, growing things, playing an instrument etc. Re-ex plore these aspects of your creative self.
    'Every child is an artist. The problem is how to remain an artist once one grows up.' – *Pablo Picasso*
2. Enrol for an evening class to develop your creativity.
3. Visit an art gallery, a theatre or a place of inspiration for your particular creative interest. Find inner healing through music and artistic expression.

Community
1. Consider: In what ways does your church/group support creativity/the arts? Is it possible that 'an artist in residence' – even for a short time – may have a deeper impact on your

local community than some of the usual church organisa
tions and activities?

2. Consider the senses – In what ways could worship become
    more 'sensual'? (e.g. hearing – music; seeing – art work;
    smells – incense, candles; etc.)
3. Support artistic expressions of spirituality, e.g. host an exhi
    bition of art – especially art which has a spiritual dimension –
    one good reason to open up your church to the wider com
    munity.
4. Find spaces for the mystery and for silence, e.g. the silences
    of a Good Friday meditation – but include such silences in
    worship regularly.

'Learn to get in touch with the silence within yourself and know
that everything in this life has a purpose.'
– *Elizabeth Kübler-Ross*

CHAPTER FIVE

Pilgrimage: People of the way

Prayer before setting sail (attributed to St Brendan the Navigator)
Shall I abandon, O King of mysteries, the soft comforts of home?
Shall I turn my back on my native land, and my face toward the sea?

Shall I put myself wholly at the mercy of God,
Without silver, without a horse, without fame and honour?
Shall I throw myself wholly on the King of Kings,
Without sword and shield, without food and drink, without a bed to lie on?

Shall I say farewell to my beautiful land, placing myself under Christ's yoke?
Shall I pour out my heart to him, confessing my manifold sins and begging forgiveness, tears streaming down my cheeks?

Shall I leave the prints of my knees on the sandy beach,
a record of my final prayer in my native land?
Shall I then suffer every kind of wound that the sea can inflict?

Shall I take my tiny coracle across the wide, sparkling ocean?
O King of the glorious Heaven, shall I go of my own choice upon the sea?

O Christ, will you help me on the wild waves?[1]

1. Pilgrimage in the Celtic Church

It is hard for us today to fully appreciate what it must have been like for the Celtic Christians who left behind their kin and country to set out, for the sake of the gospel, as wandering ascetics into a largely unmapped, unknown world which held all sorts of dangers around every corner. The pilgrim of today has the comfort of the travel itinerary, the knowledge of places to stay – booked well ahead – and a mobile phone to keep in touch. There were no such luxuries for the Celtic pilgrim, and yet *peregrinatio* or pilgrimage is one of the most important features of Celtic Christianity. For a people who had a very strong sense of place and kinship connection, to go out on pilgrimage was a very costly form of discipleship – almost a mini-death.

In her book *A World Made Whole*, Esther De Waal outlines three types of Celtic martyrdom:

1. Red Martyrdom: separation from the soul at death (mar tyrdom by sword or fire was very rare in the Celtic churches.
2. Green Martyrdom: separation from one's desires (penance as a spiritual exercise was widely practised).
3. White Martyrdom: separation from one's beloved home land (self-imposed exile was common and very painful for these home lovers).[2]

It is clear from Celtic monastic writings, such as the prayer at the beginning of this chapter, that pilgrimage was far more than just a physical journey, hard though that was. It was, most importantly, an inner journey, leaving behind all that was familiar, including one's kinship identity – literally becoming a 'nobody' for the sake of the gospel. It has echoes of Philippians 2 where it says that Christ 'emptied himself, taking the form of a servant'. It is this same attitude of *kenosis* in which the Celtic pilgrim set out, trusting in God alone. In a sense pilgrimage was a 'sacramental' journey – an outward and visible sign of an inward and spiritual grace.

2. The Bible and Nomadic Spirituality
The challenge of pilgrimage as the early church in Ireland practised it is, I believe, a powerful source of inspiration for the contemporary spiritual path. This is because it calls us to recollect and rediscover a central practice of the Christian faith which has been largely sidelined as the church has become a more settled and organised institution with its structures and buildings.

The practice of pilgrimage calls us to reconnect with a more 'nomadic' spirituality – the sort of spirituality that is willing to leave the safety zone of familiarity, and to go out on a journey of spiritual discovery, open to where God wants to guide us. This is a journey in the spirit of Brendan the Navigator, Columba of

Iona, and Abraham of old, of whom the Bible says, 'He set out not knowing where he was going' (Hebrews 11:8).

The call to nomadic spirituality, to *peregrinatio*, is a call to openness, flexibility, a perpetual faith, and an ultimate trust in the God of the Exodus and of new beginnings.

It was also a central aspect of the life of Jesus, the wandering preacher who 'had no place to lay his head' (Matthew 8:20). In the gospel Jesus says, 'There is no one who has left house or brothers or sisters or mother or father or children or fields for my sake and the sake of the gospel who will not receive a hundredfold in this age ... and in the age to come, everlasting life' (Mark 10: 29-30). In addition, the first Christians in the book of the Acts of the Apostles are called People of the Way, (Acts 9:2, 19:23, 22:4, 24:5, 24:14, 24:22) reflecting their belief in Christ, 'the Way, the Truth and the Life' (John 14:6) – but also that they perceived their faith as a 'journey' with Christ.

3. The 'Thin' Places of pilgrimage today

In the world today many people are rediscovering the ancient places of pilgrimage and making journeys to these sacred sites. Celtic Christianity spoke of them as 'Thin Places' because in these places – like Jacob's experience in the wilderness (Genesis 28:10-22) – the presence of God was so strong that it seemed as if there was only a thin veil between this world and the world of the Spirit.

Places like Iona, Glendalough, Lindisfarne, Nendrum, Skellig Michael, among others, are 'thin places' of inspiration for the spiritual journey.

The Centre for Celtic Spirituality in Armagh is fortunate to have access to a wonderful ancient heritage locally. The Anglican cathedral is on a hill overlooking the narrow circular streets of the city which has a history of 1,500 years of Christianity. Within the cathedral, along with the Christian symbols, are elements of an ancient past, including 'The Tandragee Man', 3,000 years old who represents *Nuadha* of the silver arm, ruler of the *Tuatha Dé Danann*. About two miles away is the fascinating pre-Christian site of Navan (*Emain Macha*), the earliest capital of Ulster, dating from the Iron Age, where archaeological excavations in the 1960s uncovered all sorts of objects – including the skull of a Barbary ape and a long horn, richly decorated in Celtic style, called the Loughnashade Horn – one of the oldest surviving Irish musical instruments. All of this reminds us of the spiritual traditions of our ancestors and of a world St Patrick would have found familiar.

The Centre for Celtic Spirituality welcomes those who come from many parts of the world, seeking something deeper – roots for their spiritual journey. Many share experiences of how God has spoken to them at unexpected times along the journey, sometimes about people or issues in their lives creating difficulty or obstacles in their spiritual path. Sometimes these insights come as a revelation – when everything becomes clear and comes into focus. Sometimes they happen out-of-doors, at the old wells, Celtic monastic sites or at the high crosses. They are 'thin places' and 'thin experiences'.

4. The insights which pilgrimage can bring

In setting out on pilgrimage today we may not face the same physical hazards and hardships as the Celtic Christians in ancient times, and yet there is still the opportunity for an inward journey offered by the 'shift of perspective' which pilgrimage brings. By having the courage to leave the familiar surroundings, people and routines, we provide opportunity for encountering new understandings, experiences and insights.

This shift of perspective is expressed beautifully in a poem called 'For the Traveller', by John O'Donohue in which he says:

> When you travel,
> A new silence
> Goes with you,
> And if you listen,
> You will hear
> What your heart would
> Love to say.[3]

On pilgrimage we are able to be more receptive to the new environment in which we find ourselves. There is a heightened sense of expectation and, to gain the most from the experience, we need to be open to 'going with the flow' of the sacred journey.

Someone once said that the other side of 'sacred' is 'scared'. It is a risk to journey for, as the French writer André Gide once said, 'One does not discover new lands without consenting to lose sight of the shore for a very long time.'

In 2009 Revd Ray Simpson of the international community of Aidan and Hilda, Holy Island, Lindisfarne, came to Armagh and told us a memorable story about St Brendan the Navigator. In their small coracle on the ocean Brendan and his companions were rowing hard into the face of the wind. When the wind ceased and calm descended they felt dispirited, wanting to give up the voyage. Then one of Brendan's companions said, 'Let's abandon ourselves to the voyage, and let the wind blow us where it will.'

This is the true spirit of the nomad: to stop rowing – stop trying so hard – and go with the flow of the Holy Spirit.

I remember speaking about this with the late Derek Bingham, because he always ended his e-mails with,'In the service of the Easy Yoke'. It was a reference to the words of Jesus, 'My yoke is easy and my burden is light' (Matthew 11:30). Derek said: 'Think about it – if your yoke is heavy, whose yoke is it that you're carrying?'

Of course the opportunity to go on pilgrimage is not available to everyone, for all sorts of reasons, yet the nomadic spirit is an inner journey of the heart which one can develop in any place or at any time of life.

Often these deepest insights are prompted by difficult life experiences – grief, illness, relationship breakdown – which create a sense of 'feeling lost' in a person. There's an old prayer of the Breton fishermen which says, 'Lord, I am sailing on a wide, wide sea; please guide my little boat for me.'

Experiences of suffering are difficult pilgrimage journeys. Cut off from the familiar anchors of life, we find ourselves depending on God in a new way – it's a 'thin place' and a 'thin experience' – in a sense it's the white martyrdom of the Celtic Christians.

All of these insights and inspirations come from the pilgrimaging spirit of Celtic Christianity and the challenge is to open up our hearts to the new perspectives and experiences to which God is seeking to guide us.

Nomadic spirituality is a call to be truly People of The Way, to have the courage to take the risk of leaving the comfortable and the familiar – our usual 'rut' – to 'go with the flow' of God's Holy Spirit and follow the urgency of the Call that is there in the depths of our hearts – if we have the courage to truly listen to our hearts.

The wonderful Brazilian writer, Paulo Coelho, who wrote a book about the Camino de Santiago de Compostela called *The Pilgrimage*, made a very interesting observation – in the spirit of the Celtic pilgrim – in his book *Like the Flowing River*. The short story is called 'In Miami Harbour' and in it his friend asks him if he remembers the film *The Ten Commandments*.

He replies: 'Of course I do. At one point, Moses – Charlton Heston – lifts up his rod, the waters part, and the children of Israel cross over.'

His friend then says: 'In the Bible it's different, for there God says to Moses: "Tell the Israelites to go forward" (Exodus 14:15). And only afterwards does he tell Moses to lift up his rod, and then the red sea parts.'

He concludes: 'It is only courage on the path itself that makes the path appear.'[4]

Pilgrimage: Practical Inspirations

Individual

1. Examine your own life and your ways of thinking. Are you 'stuck in a rut?' Have you 'spiritual arthritis?' What would challenge your sense of the familiar? It could be attending worship at a different church denomination some Sunday or reading a book on a subject that you know will challenge your usual opinions.
2. Be open to the call of your own heart. What is it that you are truly passionate about? God has given you a particular gift/ gifts – discern what they are through recognising the passions of your heart.
3. Read the poem 'The Journey' by Mary Oliver. Find some time to reflect on your own life. Is there anything that may be holding you back from fulfilling the vocation(s) of your heart? In what ways, if any, does this poem speak to you about your life?

4. Plan a journey or a pilgrimage or a retreat, even a day retreat
    – space to discern the call.

> 'True life is lived when tiny changes occur.'
> – *Leo Tolstoy*

Community
1. Seek a link-relationship with another group or church de
    nomination that is quite different from yours. Perhaps even a
    different faith community? Or an international link?
2. Move out of your church building and worship outdoors
    some Sunday – perhaps in the grounds of an ancient, ruined
    church (permission may be required), a historic place, an old
    well or a place of natural beauty. If it's close by, you could do
    a short walking pilgrimage.
3. Initiate changes of perspective by inviting speakers with a
    difference; if you have a study group, study books which
    come from a different perspective. Encourage continual re
    flection on the journey your group/church community is on.
4. Organise a group or church pilgrimage, for example, to Iona
    or Glendalough..

CHAPTER SIX

The Other World:
Death, saints and angels

'There is a presence who walks the road of life with you.
This presence accompanies your every moment …
The name of this presence is death.'
– *John O'Donohue*[1]

If there is one subject that today's western culture finds particularly difficult to face up to, it is everything connected with ageing, dying and death. Perhaps because of the diminishing space for the spiritual and the increasing importance of materialism, there is an obsession with eternal youthfulness, a disrespect for the gifts and wisdom of old age and a deep-seated fear and denial of the fact of death.

But to live in denial about the inevitability of death brings its own problems, many of which I have encountered during my years in the church's ordained ministry, having officiated at the funeral services of hundreds of people.

For example, because the subject of death is treated as a kind of taboo, the grief that naturally arises through separation and loss is often suppressed. It seems there are few meaningful rituals or socially acceptable ways of dealing with grief. When someone is bereaved they discover that sometimes neighbours will even cross over to the other side of the road in order to avoid meeting and having to address the subject of death.

For the person who has lost a loved one, it is often difficult to speak of them again for fear of causing embarrassment or – in the case of speaking to someone recently bereaved – of awakening a volcano of grief. In speaking about the dead, 'safe' words and phrases are used such as 'passed on' or 'passed away' or 'at rest' instead of 'dead' – which is perceived to be unacceptably stark.

So, in effect, gone means forgotten.

The exception to this may be some of the rituals in the Roman Catholic Church, which has practices such as 'graveyard

Sunday', the 'month's mind' Mass and other anniversary
Masses for the remembrance of the dead. But in the 'reformed'
churches the whole issue can be complicated further by particular theological traditions which teach that praying to or for the
dead is a sin.

Yet just because a person has died, doesn't mean that they
cease to have any connection with the living – indeed a dead
person can continue to exercise influence over the living. Indeed
this can be a very positive influence, bringing help and encouragement to the person, who feels a sense of being 'looked after'
by their loved one who has gone to the next life.

But, it can also be a very negative influence.

To share an example of this from my own ministry, a lady
came to see me who was full of resentment and hatred against a
man who had ill-treated and abused her for years. The man was
now dead, yet this lady still carried the scars and a heavy burden of unforgiveness. In a negative way she was still connected
to this man – in fact her deep resentment was, in itself, a strong
tie of attachment. In addition, her sadness and anger, which she
held deep within herself, was affecting her own health and well-
being. After a period of compassionate listening this lady came
to a stage in her understanding where she clearly realised that in
order to be free and well again, she needed to 'cut the tie' that
was binding her. Together we worked on several approaches to
achieving that 'cutting of the tie', which involved a Eucharist
and anointing with the oil of healing, all of which ultimately
was radically effective in bringing release and healing to this
lady.

Influences like this in the lives of people can be very real –
they can even affect whole families (some would say whole soci-
eties) with negative influences coming through a family tree of
'ancestral voices'. To deal with these kinds of connections with
the 'Otherworld' we need to be able to talk more freely and with
less inhibition about the dead, and overcome our estrangement
from this most certain of events for us all – our own death.

This is where the traditions and practices of Celtic Christianity surrounding death and the next life, which are full of rich
and helpful meaning, may have much to contribute to our contemporary culture.

To begin with, the early church in Ireland had a strong sense that the otherworld was not 'a land far, far away' or 'away far beyond Jordan', to quote some familiar Christian hymns – instead it was a familiar part of everyday life.

In *Anamchara* John O'Donohue states: 'The Celtic tradition had a refined sense of the miracle of death ... For the Celts the eternal world was so close to the natural world that death was not seen as a terribly destructive or threatening event. When you enter the eternal world, you are going home to where no shadow, pain or darkness can ever touch you again.'[2]

Death was not something to be feared and dreaded, but an inevitable part of life and a rite of passage to the eternal home of the soul.

Celtic Christianity, drawing on the teachings of scripture, understood this eternal home to be the place where the soul returned home to God from where it had come (Ecclesiastes 12:7) – the place also of the saints and the angels. In their liturgies and practices surrounding death and dying, there are references to the final journey of the soul and the importance of allowing the soul to depart in peace – for the living to 'let go' of the loved one, so that the soul can be guided by the angels into the fullness of the Divine Presence.

So in this final chapter of *Sacred Living*, I want to examine some of the traditions of Celtic Christianity in relation to death and the 'Otherworld', and consider inspirations for us today regarding Sacred Dying.

The dying and the dead

At the heart of the Christian faith is belief in life after death. Through the resurrection of Christ the power of death is defeated (1 Corinthians 15:53-57) and the gateway is opened into God's presence which, in its fullness, is heaven itself. The Bible describes heaven as 'a place where there is no more death and where mourning and crying and pain will be no more.' (Revelation 21:4) – the place of the ultimate healing of the soul.

The Bible also describes heaven as the place of the saints and the angels and in the Celtic tradition this 'otherworld' was a part of daily life – as were its inhabitants, whose presence surrounds us.

I heard a lovely example of this recently at a talk given by Fr J. J. Ó Ríordáin, a well known writer on Celtic Spirituality, at the St Bronagh's School of Celtic Studies in Rostrevor. This group is an ecumenical gathering of Christian people, inspired by Celtic Spirituality, and led by Revd Canon Dermot Jameson and Fr J. J. Ó Ríordáin.

He told a story about being on a pastoral visit to an elderly housebound lady in Dundalk. As she lived alone he asked her if she felt lonely or isolated. She replied by pointing around the walls to the pictorial images of the Blessed Virgin, St Michael and the Sacred Heart of Jesus and exclaimed, 'How could I be lonely when I have our Lord, His blessed Mother and all the saints and angels here with me? Sure I'm surrounded by them all!'

The Cloud of Witnesses, the Guardian Angel and the Caim
This lady had a keen sense of what the Bible calls 'the cloud of witnesses' in Hebrews chapters 11 and 12. Here there is a list of all the ancestors of the Jewish faith and then chapter 12 begins: 'Since we are surrounded by so great a cloud of witnesses, let us lay aside every weight and the sin that clings so closely, and let us run with perseverance the race that is set before us.'

From this perspective, the presence of the ancestors, the saints and the angels, surrounds the living as a source of help and encouragement.

For example, they had an understanding about the particular role of the Guardian Angel whose task it is to take care of the particular human being they have been assigned to by God. Jesus himself seems to make reference to the role of the Guardian Angel when he says 'Take care that you do not despise one of these little ones, for I tell you, in heaven their angels continually see the face of my Father in heaven' (Matthew 18:10).

A beautiful practice is described by a lady, who was reared in Irish-speaking Donegal, regarding the help of the angels to humankind. In her book *Celtic Wisdom and Contemporary Living*, Phyllida Anam-Aire says:

My nanny always invited the spirit people to the table when we ate together. The chair was put there for them, and no one could sit on it! These spirit people were referred to as *daoine naoifa* – 'the holy ones'. It was believed that at birth and death these unseen guests came to assist humans. At birth their task was to re-echo the note that enticed the soul to earth. It was believed that the same angel or helper re-echoed the same note in a higher octave when the soul departed from the body.[3]

This reminds me of the lovely practice of 'the unseen guest at every meal' – being thankful to God for your food, and recognising the presence of Christ by placing a chair for the unseen guest.

Celtic Christianity also had a practice called 'The Caim' which was a prayer of encircling through which the awareness of the Divine power and presence was affirmed. It was also an invocation of protection against negative or evil powers.

In his book *The Path of Light*, David Adams comments: 'Very often to make the Caim you would face east and raise your right hand and point forwards. Then you would turn slowly in a sunwise or clockwise direction until you had completed a circle.'[4] While doing this, the prayer of encircling or encompassing was said, invoking the power of the saints, the angels and the Holy Trinity.

The following is an example of such a prayer of encompassment from the *Carmina Gadelica*:

The holy Apostles' guarding,
The gentle martyrs' guarding
The nine angels' guarding,
Be cherishing me, be aiding me.

The quiet Brigid's guarding,
The gentle Mary's guarding,
The warrior Michael's guarding,
Be shielding me, be aiding me.

The God of the elements' guarding,
The loving Christ's guarding,
The holy Spirit's guarding,
Be cherishing me, be aiding me.[5]

In the Celtic monastic communities there was an under-standing that the living and the dead belonged together which was especially evident in the practice of burying the monks where they had lived. For example, at Nendrum the graves of the monks are in the central enclosure, so the community con-sisted not only of the living, but also of those who had died – they remained a part of the community in which they had lived. Seán Ó Duinn in *Where Three Streams Meet* comments: 'Often nowadays the church stands several miles away from the grave-yard, so that this sense of unity with the dead is forgotten.'[6]

The Wake and the leading of the soul

This understanding that the presence of the saints and the an-gels surround the living as a source of help and encouragement has continued to be reflected in some of the practices surround-ing death and dying in Celtic regions.

For example, John O'Donohue speaks about the Irish tradi-tion of the wake in his book *Anamchara*. He says: 'Its ritual af-fords the soul plenty of time to take its leave. The soul does not leave the body abruptly; this is a slow leave-taking … It is im-portant not to leave the dead person on his own. Funeral homes are cold, clinical places. If at all possible when the person dies, they should be left in their familiar surroundings so that they can make this deeper transition in a comfortable, easy and se-cure way … The person who has entered the voyage of death needs more in-depth care.'[7]

This approach also gives the family and loved ones the space and opportunity to take their farewell and to allow the soul to depart in peace.

Death in the Celtic tradition was not a journey to be feared, but a transition to the place of eternal rest of the soul. This prayer from the *Carmina Gadelica* sees death as 'going home' – the final homecoming of the soul – and immersed in the natural rhythms of the earth.

> I am going home with thee
> To thy home! to thy home!
> I am going home with thee
> To thy home of winter.

I am going home with thee
To thy home! to thy home!
I am going home with thee
To thy home of autumn, of spring and of summer.

I am going home with thee,
Thou child of my love,
To thine eternal bed,
To thy perpetual sleep.

I am going home with thee,
Thou child of my love,
To the dear Son of blessings,
To the Father of grace.[8]

Leading the Soul
This tradition of 'death-blessing' was practised by Celtic Christians and is described by Esther De Waal as follows:

> A soul-friend, the 'anam-chara', almost always a lay person,
> would sing or intone the soul peace over the dying person, and
> all present would join in beseeching the three persons of the
> Godhead and all the saints of heaven to receive the departing
> soul. During the prayer the soul-friend would make the sign of
> the cross with the right thumb over the lips of the dying ...[9]

The following is an example from the *Carmina Gadelica* of
'The Soul Leading' prayer.

Thou King of the City of Heaven. Amen.

Since thou O Christ it was who bought'st this soul,
Be its peace on Thine own keeping. Amen.

And may the strong Michael, high king of the angels,
Be preparing the path before this soul, O God. Amen.

Oh! The strong Michael in peace with thee, soul,
And preparing for thee the way to the kingdom of the Son of
God. Amen.[10]

The eternal soul

In his book *Before we say Goodbye: Preparing for a Good death* Ray Simpson advises 'Make death your Anamchara. Quoting from John O'Donohue's book *Anamchara* he says: 'Death is the great wound in the universe, the root of all fear and negativity. Friendship with our death would enable us to celebrate the eternity of the soul which death cannot touch...'[11]

Following the example of the early church in Ireland, this is about becoming familiar with the 'Otherworld' and opening our inner perception to the Sacred Presence in every aspect of living.

In the life of Jesus he was continually aware of the presence of the Father (John 8:28-29), he was assisted by angelic beings (Mark 1:13), he conversed with the dead during his 'transfiguration' experience when he met with Moses and Elijah (Mark 9:4) and he had made his own preparations for his death (Matthew 16:21).

The practices of Celtic Christianity encourage us to reflect on death and dying and the 'Otherworld' with an approach that is healing and helpful for the twenty-first century – to look differently at the meaning of the death of our loved ones and at our own death when it comes.

All of these ancient traditions speak to us of deeper wisdom, help and inspiration along the journey from life to death.

John O'Donohue had many wise insights about the path towards death and beyond, and he himself died suddenly and at a relatively young age – but he was well-prepared for the journey.

These are some words from his poem of blessing for death:

Entering Death
When you come to die,
May it be after a long life.

May you be tranquil
Among those who care for you.
May your going be sheltered
And your welcome assured.

May your soul smile
In the embrace
Of your Anamchara.[12]

The Other World: Practical inspirations

Individual

1. Become more aware of your own ancestors – their genes are also in you. Be aware of their life stories and what character istics you might have inherited from them. If possible, collect their photographs and keep them in a special place. Visit their graves.
2. Review your life – Ray Simpson has a very helpful approach to this in his book *Before We Say Goodbye* (pp 32-36). This exer cise helps us to be clearer about what we perceive to be our achievements, our life path and what aspirations wait to be fulfilled for us.
3. Volunteer in your local Hospice.
4. Consider making preparations for your own death – make a will, consider requests for where/how you will die, the fu neral service, the place of burial/cremation and other such considerations.

Community

1. As in chapter three, find new festivals that truly connect with peoples' lives.
2. Find out and celebrate the history of your community/ church. Remember those who have been a part of your com munity in the past, and find ways of telling their stories.
3. Keep a *Memorial Book* (different from a 'funeral register') in a prominent place in which all deaths are recorded annually. This can be a helpful record for the church/group and also useful as part of the liturgy at All Saints' Tide.
4. Encourage reflection, perhaps as part of a study group series, on difficult subjects such as dying, death, what happens after death, bereavement and ethical issues such as euthanasia or assisted dying. This provides opportunity for people to share experiences and to think more deeply about these issues in relation to their own faith.

Conclusion

In my childhood years we lived in an old white-washed traditional low-set Irish farmhouse inherited by my father – along
with 30 acres of land – from his mother. It was set in the heart of
the country, at the end of a long, narrow lane, flanked by high
hedges, where the birds nested in the springtime.

It was a simple living, where my father kept dairy cows and
knew each one by name and we drank the sweet milk they pro-
duced and ate home-grown vegetables and eggs from the chick-
ens in the field-pen ('free-range' and 'organic' were unheard of,
because everything was free-range and organic!). In the summer
we harvested soft fruit and had a few days holiday at the nearest
County Down coastline.

We eaked out a living in simple ways with family closeness,
no technology (until the telephone and the television arrived in
the 70s), or central heating and enjoyed the visits of neighbours
on a winter's evening talking round the open fire.

We celebrated the annual festivals – Christmas, Easter,
Whitsun, Hallowe'en and birthdays – with enthusiasm, and
through the seasons life had a natural and dependable rhythm.

I can now see that these childhood connections with the natural rhythms of the earth's cycles were foundational in drawing
me towards Celtic spirituality. Somehow in all the changes in
our social ways of living over the past forty years we have lost
these vital connections and have impoverished our own souls.

Hannah Cunningham, in the foreword to *Celtic Wisdom and
Contemporary Living*, puts it like this:

> We live in a modern world heavily influenced by thought, and
> technological skills, which have brought us to the point of think-
> ing it is unnecessary to have the powers of the universe within
> us … We have so often failed to maintain communion with the
> deeper powers, with the birds that soar, the winds that howl

their presence, the mountains that hold the stories of the past, the flowers that share their bounty of colour and fragrance. Where is the validation in us these days, from the ritual integration with the liturgy of the seasons, and the turning of the days, from day to night and back again. These transitions we once knew as sacred … We have, in essence, trivialised our existence by losing our sense of soul. Without the assistance of soul … we do not know where our power point is. The world we have created, both inside and out, can take us no further, and we need to return again, be awakened, and reawakened to our soul's calling.[1]

Listening to the soul's calling is what has led many people to travel from all over the world to Ireland, and to Armagh, to seek out an experience of Celtic spirituality for themselves. There are, of course, many ways of searching, in addition to Celtic spirituality, but in the end only one destination – the healing of the soul through relationship with the Sacred Presence. Along the journey Celtic spirituality reconnects us with the roots of ancient wisdom in various ways, some of which are as follows:

1. In its understanding of creation, hospitality and creative spirituality, Celtic spirituality enables healing of relationship with ourselves, one another and with all creation in celebration of the fullness of our sacred identity. It is a coat-of-many-colours approach to spirituality.
2. Celtic spirituality practises harmony with the rhythms of the earth, marking the seasons of the year with simplicity and care and contributing deep meaning to life.
3. Celtic spirituality encourages flexibility, compassionate openness and a pilgrim heart, following the example of Christ and of the early Christians and the Hebrews of old in The Way of the Nomad.
4. Celtic spirituality inspires us in practical and ethical ways to 'bless our world into sacredness' by being conscious of the Sacred in every part of life. It is a calling to 'follow the road less travelled' in contrast and challenge to the materialistic culture of our age.

Paulo Coelho calls this vocation 'being a warrior of light'. Romans 13:12 also echoes the same vocation when it says: 'Put on the armour of light'.

In *Benedictus* John O'Donohue speaks of this vocation in these words:

> Sometimes when we look out, the world seems so dark. War, violence, hunger and misery seem to abound. This makes us anxious and helpless. What can I do in my private little corner of life that could have any effect on the march of world events? The usual answer is: nothing. We then decide to do what we can for our own, and leave the great events to their domain. Thus, we opt out, and join the largest majority in the world: those who acquiesce. Believing ourselves to be helpless, we hand over all our power to forces and systems outside us that then act in our names; they go on to put their beliefs into action, and ironically these actions are often sinister and destructive. We live in times when the call to full and aware citizenship could not be more urgent. We need to rediscover the careless courage, yet devastating simplicity, of the little boy who in the middle of the numbed multitude, in naïve Socratic fashion, blurts out: 'But the emperor has no clothes.' When spoken, the word of truth can bring down citadels of falsity.[2]

May the power and inspiration of Celtic spirituality enable us to be channels of truth, Sacred blessing and eternal Presence to the world.

A Traditional Celtic blessing
May the wind be always at your back,
May the sun shine warm upon your face,
May the rain fall softly on your fields,
And until we meet again,
May God hold you in the hollow of his hand.

Bibliography

Adam, David, *The Cry of the Deer: Meditations on the hymn of St Patrick*, SPCK, 1987.

Adam, David, *The Path of Light*, SPCK, 2009.

Anam-Aire, Phyllida, *Celtic Wisdom and Contemporary Living*, Findhorn Press, 2007.

Bradley, Ian, *The Celtic Way*, DLT, 1993.

Cameron, Julia, *The Artist's Way*, Pan Books, 1993.

Carmichael, Alexander, *Carmina Gadelica*, Edinburgh, 1994.

De Waal, Esther, *The Celtic Vision*, DLT, 1988.

De Waal, Esther, *The Celtic Way of Prayer: The rediscovery of the religious imagination*, Canterbury Press, 2010.

De Waal, Esther, *World Made Whole: Rediscovering the Celtic Tradition*, Harper Collins, 1991.

Housden, Roger (ed), *Ten Poems to Change Your Life*, Hodder and Stoughton, 2003.

Hull, E. (ed), *The Poem Book of the Gael*, Chatto and Windus, London, 1912.

Low, Mary, *Celtic Christianity and Nature: Early Irish and Hebridean Traditions*, Blackstaff Press, 1996.

MacMaster, Johnston, *A Passion for Justice: Social Ethics in the Celtic Tradition*, Dunedin, 2008.

Macquarrie, John, *Paths in Spirituality*, Morehouse Group, August, 1993.

Moore, Thomas, *Care of the Soul*, Piatkus Books, 1992.

Newell, John Philip, *Christ of the Celts*, John Wiley and Sons, 2008.

O'Donoghue, Noel Dermot, *The Mountain Behind the Mountain: Aspects of the Celtic Tradition*, T&T Clark, 1993.

O'Donohue, John, *Anam Chara*, Bantam Press, 1997.

O'Donohue, John, *Benedictus*, Bantam Press, 2007.

O'Donohue, John, *Divine Beauty: The Invisible Embrace*, Bantam Press, 2003.

O'Donohue, John, *Eternal Echoes: Exploring our hunger to belong*, Bantam Press, 1998.

Ó Duinn, Seán, *Where Three Streams Meet*, Columba Press, 2000.

Power, Rosemary, *The Celtic Quest*, Columba Press, 2010.

Sheldrake, Philip, *Living Between Worlds: place and journey in Celtic Spirituality*, DLT, 1995.

Simpson, Ray, *Before We Say Goodbye: Preparing for a good death*, Harper Collins, 2001.

Van de Weyer, Robert, *Celtic Prayers*, Hunt and Thorpe, 1997.

Further Resources

The Centre for Celtic Spirituality is based in Armagh, Northern Ireland. It is a shared charitable project with a management committee that has members from the Methodist church, the Presbyterian church, the Roman Catholic church, the Anglican church, the Quakers and the Mennonites.
Its aims are:

- To share the ancient heritage of Celtic Spirituality, so evident in Armagh, with the rest of the world.
- To inspire others – of all faiths and none – on their spiritual journey through the power of Celtic spirituality.
- To bring together Christian churches in a spirit of peace, respect and understanding.

The Centre for Celtic Spirituality has a website, www.celtic-spirituality.net, on which its programme and work can be viewed.

Academic Study
The International Community of Aidan and Hilda (www.aidanandhilda.org) offers an E-Studies course and sabbatical study guidelines.

The University of Lampeter in Wales offers an MA in Celtic Christianity – see www.lamp.ac.uk

To investigate the academic background to the contemporary phenomenon of Celtic spirituality read *The Celtic Quest* by Rosemary Power, Columba Press, 2010.

Other themes
1. *Personal Hospitality (Creation/A Way of Living)*
   Read the writings of Louise Hay – in particular, *Love Yourself, Heal your life*. See www.healyourlife.com

2. *Life-changing simplicity (A Way of Living)*
   Lane, John, *Timeless Simplicity: Creative living in a consumer
   society*, Green Books, 2001.

   Van Eyk McCain, Marion, *The Lilypad List: 7 steps to the simple
   life*, Findhorn Press, 2004.

Also be inspired by the simple lives of people like Fr Bede
Griffiths and Thomas Merton.

3. *Releasing your own creativity (Creative Spirituality)*
   Cameron, Julia, *The Artist's Way*, Pan Books, 1993.
   — *The Sound of Paper*, Penguin, 2004.

Both books are wonderfully inspiring to anyone wishing to find
practical guidance for starting the creative process.

4. *Facing death (The Other World)*
   Simpson, Ray, *Before We Say Goodbye: Preparing for a good
   death*, Harper Collins, 2001.

Notes

INTRODUCTION

1. Sheldrake, Philip, *Living Between Worlds: place and journey in Celtic Spirituality*, DLT, 1995, pp 1-8.
2. O'Donohue John, *Benedictus*, Bantam Press, 2007, p 53.

CHAPTER ONE

1. The Irish Peace Centres are a consortium involving An Teach Bán in County Donegal, Corrymeela in County Antrim, and Glencree in County Wicklow. See www.irishpeacecentres.org
2. O'Donoghue, Noel Dermot, *The Mountain Behind the Mountain: Aspects of the Celtic Tradition*, T&T Clark, 1993, pp 30-31.
3. Macquarrie, John, *Paths in Spirituality*, Morehouse Group, August 1993, pp 122-3.
4. Van de Weyer Robert, *Celtic Prayers*, Hunt and Thorpe, 1997, p 17. *(This poem comes from a very ancient source – attributed to Amergin, hundreds of years before Christ.)*

CHAPTER TWO

1. Newell, John Philip, *Christ of the Celts*, John Wiley and Sons, 2008, pp 3-4.
2. De Mello, Anthony, *The Heart of the Enlightened*, Fount paperbacks, 1989, pp 98-99.
3. Moore, Thomas, *Care of the Soul*, Piatkus Books, 1992, p ix.

CHAPTER THREE

1. O'Donohue, John, *Anam Chara*, Bantam Press, 1997, p 16.
2. Van de Weyer, Robert, *Celtic Prayers*, Hunt and Thorpe, 1997, p 26.
3. Ó Duinn, Seán, *Where Three Streams Meet*, Columba Press, 2000, p 77.
4. Ó Duinn, Seán, *Where Three Streams Meet*, Columba Press, 2000, p 78.
5. O'Donohue, John, *Benedictus*, Bantam Press, 2007, p 206.
6. Bradley, Ian, *The Celtic Way*, DLT, 1993, p 73.
7. O'Donohue, John, *Anam Chara*, Bantam Press, 1997, p 16.
8. Bradley, Ian, *The Celtic Way*, DLT, 1993, p 73.
9. E. Hull (ed), *The Poem Book of the Gael*, Chatto and Windus, London, 1912, p 112.

CHAPTER FOUR

1. Bradley, Ian, *The Celtic Way*, DLT, 1993, pp 73-4.
2. De Waal, Esther, *World Made Whole: Rediscovering the Celtic Tradition*, Harper Collins, 1991.
3. Cameron, Julia, *The Artist's Way*, Pan Books, 1993, p 1.
4. Giles, Richard, *At Heaven's Gate*, Canterbury Press, 2010, pp 25-6.

CHAPTER FIVE

1. Van de Weyer, Robert, *Celtic Prayers*, Hunt and Thorpe, 1997, p 20.
2. De Waal, Esther, *World Made Whole: Rediscovering the Celtic Tradition*, Harper Collins, 1991.
3. O'Donohue, John, *Benedictus*, Bantam Press, 2007, pp 69-71.
4. Coelho, Paulo, *Like the Flowing River*, Harper Collins, 2006, p 123.

CHAPTER SIX

1. O'Donohue, John, *Anam Chara*, Bantam Press, 1997, p 243.
2. O'Donohue, John, *Anam Chara*, Bantam Press, 1997, p 250.
3. Anam-Aire, Phyllida, *Celtic Wisdom and Contemporary Living*, Findhorn Press, 2007, p 127.
4. Adam, David, *The Path of Light*, SPCK, 2009, p 81.
5. Carmichael, Alexander, *Carmina Gadelica*, Edinburgh, 1994, chapter 111, p 107.
6. Ó Duinn, Seán, *Where Three Streams Meet*, Columba Press, 2000, p 52.
7. O'Donohue, John, *Anam Chara*, Bantam Press, 1997, pp 259-60.
8. Carmichael, Alexander, *Carmina Gadelica*, Edinburgh, 1994, chapter 111, pp 379-81.
9. De Waal, Esther, *The Celtic Vision*, DLT 1988, pp 111-2.
10. Carmichael, Alexander, *Carmina Gadelica*, Edinburgh, 1994, chapter 1, p 117.
11. Simpson, Ray, *Before We Say Goodbye: Preparing for a good death*, Harper Collins, 2001, p 8.
12. O'Donohue John, *Benedictus*, Bantam Press, 2007, p 192.

CONCLUSION

1. Anam-Aire, Phyllida, *Celtic Wisdom and Contemporary Living*, Findhorn Press, 2007, p 11.
2. O'Donohue John, *Benedictus*, Bantam Press, 2007, p 224.